Unicorn Halloween
Coloring Book for Kids Ages 4-8

Copyright 2020 by Happy Harper - All rights reserved.

This document is geared towards providing exact and reliable information in regards to the topic and issue covered. The publication is sold with the idea that the publisher is not required to render an accounting, officially permitted, or otherwise, qualified services. If advice is necessary, legal or professional, a practiced individual in the profession should be ordered.

- From a Declaration of Principles which was accepted and approved equally by a Committee of the American Bar Association and a Committee of Publishers and Associations.

In no way is it legal to reproduce, duplicate, or transmit any part of this document by either electronic means or in printed format. Recording of this publication is strictly prohibited and any storage of this document is not allowed unless with written permission from the publisher. All rights reserved.

The information provided herein is stated to be truthful and consistent, in that any liability, in terms of inattention or otherwise, by any usage or abuse of any policies, processes, or directions contained within is the solitary and utter responsibility of the recipient reader. Under no circumstances will any legal responsibility or blame be held against the publisher for any reparation, damages, or monetary loss due to the information herein, either directly or indirectly.

Respective authors and companies own all copyrights not held by the publisher.

The information herein is offered for informational purposes solely and is universal as so. The presentation of the information is without a contract or any type of guarantee assurance.

The trademarks that are used are without any consent, and the publication of the trademark is without permission or backing by the trademark owner. All trademarks and brands within this book are for clarifying purposes only and are owned by the owners themselves, not affiliated with this document.

This Book Belongs to

_____

Halloween Fact #1

The word Jack o'lantern comes from the legend of Stinky Jack, who outwitted the devil himself!

Fun Unicorn Fact #1

The word unicorn means one horn and it comes from the Latin word unus meaning one and cornu meaning horn.

Halloween Fact #2

Trick or treating began from something called souling during which, poor children and adults would go door to door accepting food for prayers.

Fun Unicorn Fact #2

The unicorn's horn is said to have magical healing powers and can quickly cure wounds, sickness and even poison.

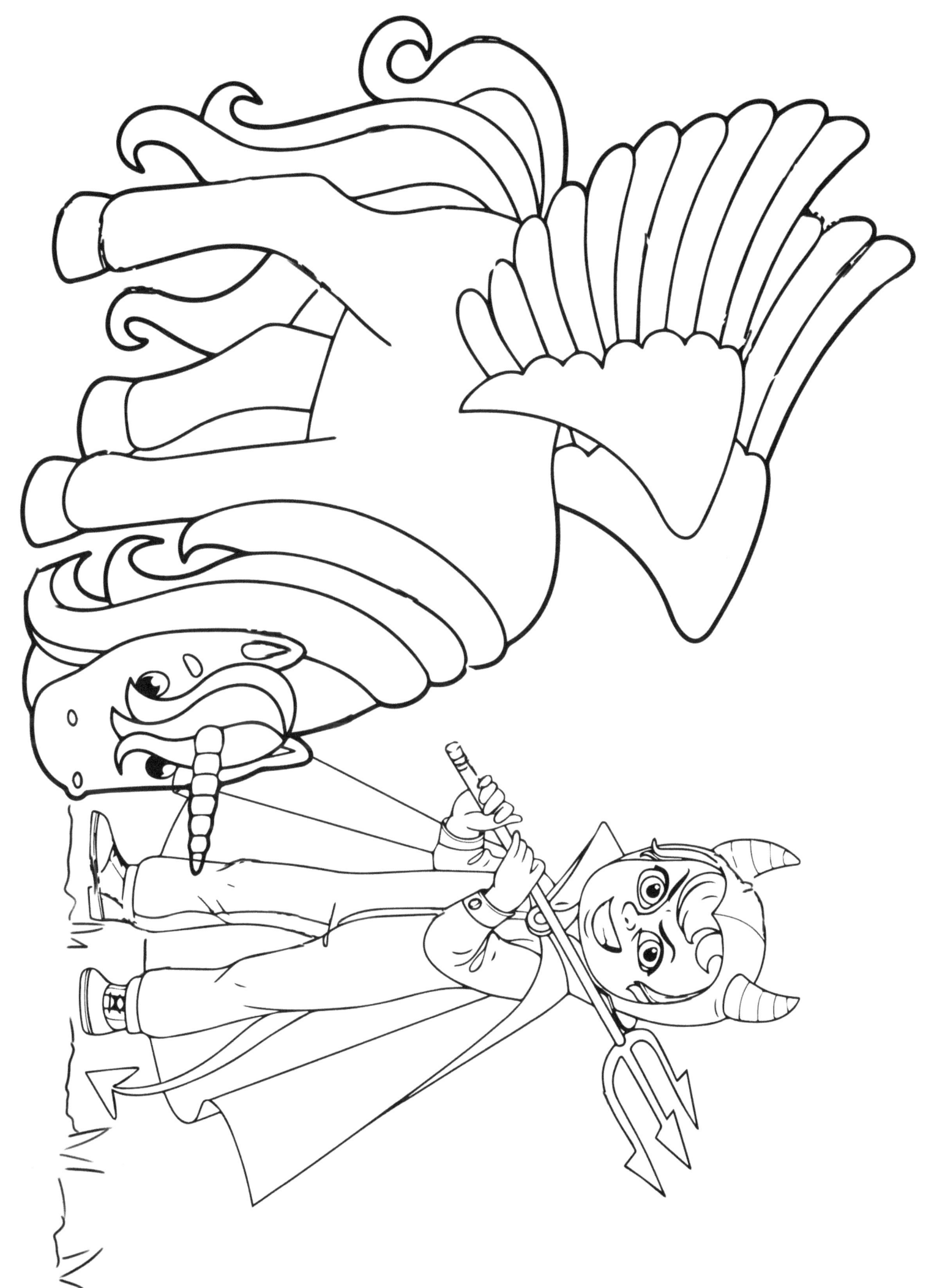

Halloween Fact #3

Halloween comes from the ancient Celtic end of harvest festival called Samhain.

Fun Unicorn Fact #3

The first written account of a unicorn is 2400 years old and was written by a Greek doctor named Ctesias who heard that there were sightings of unicorns in India.

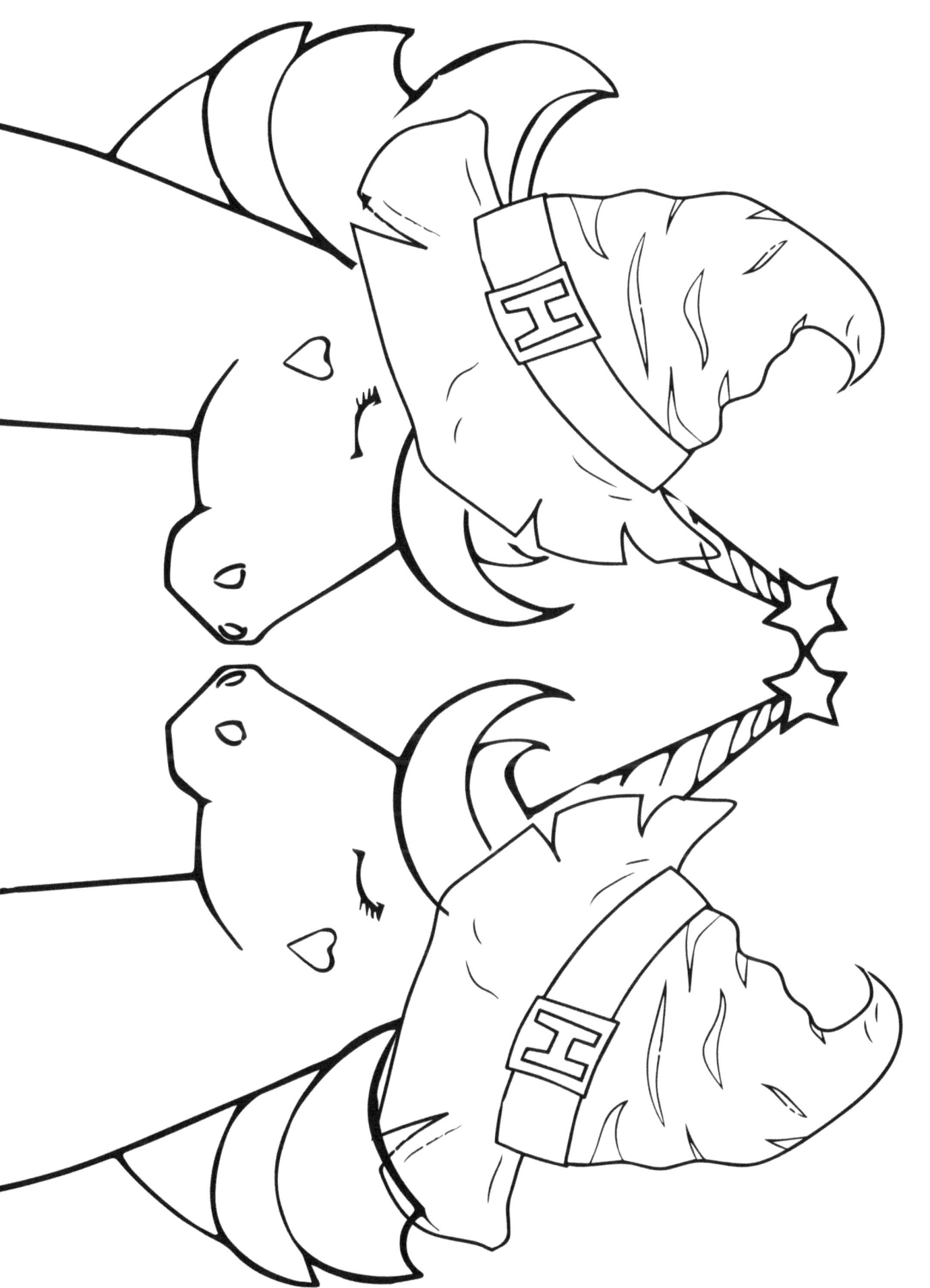

Fun Unicorn Fact #4

Narwhals are fishes that have horns and are usually called sea unicorns.

Halloween Fact #4

During the festival of Samhain, people used bonfires and a variety of costumes to supposedly ward away evil spirits.

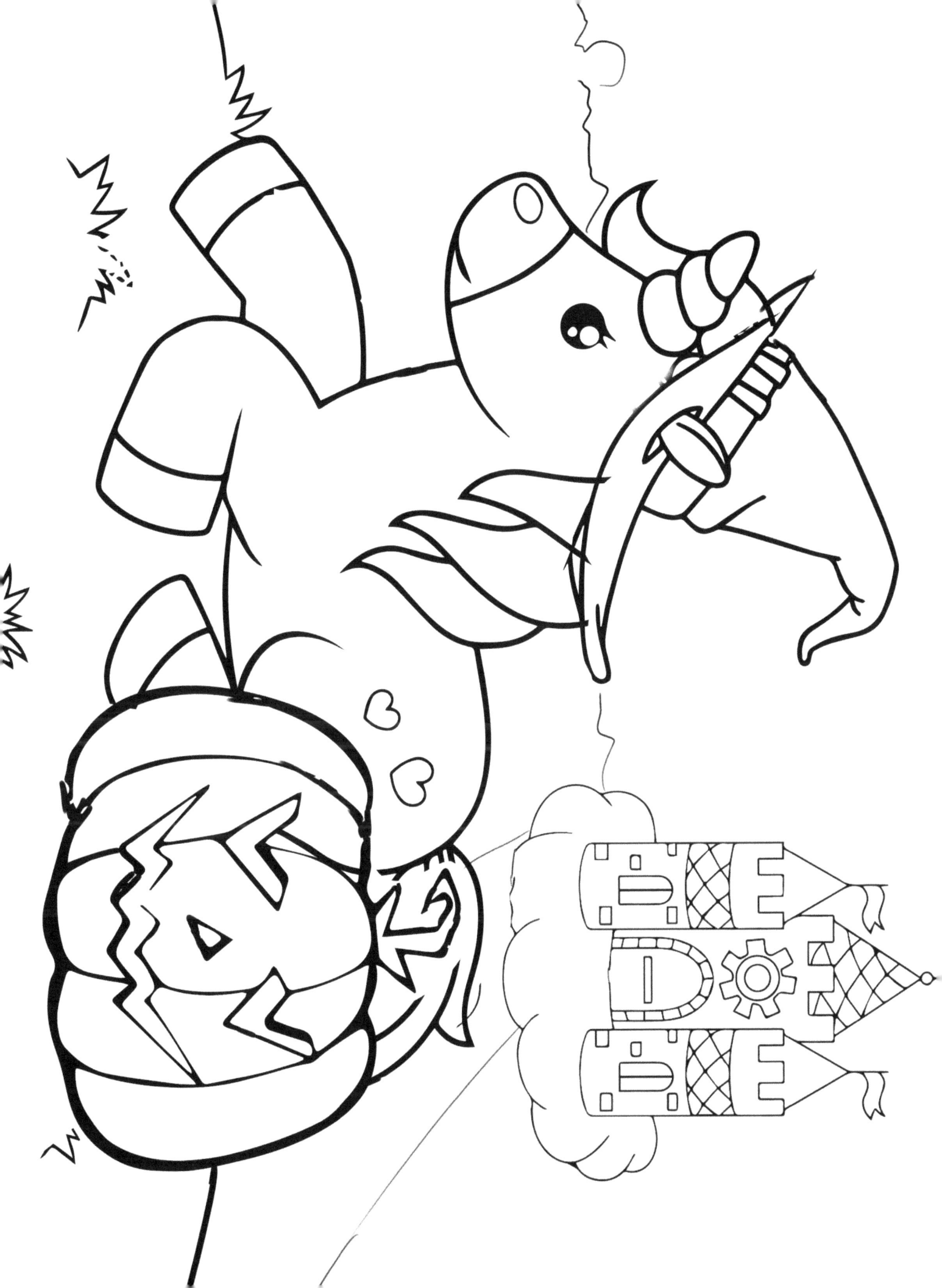

Halloween Fact #5

Trick or treating has been around since medieval times (the times of knights in shining armor and kings and queens!)

Fun Unicorn Fact #5

Unicorns were said to be so fearful that no hunter could ever catch them. You had to be a maiden with a pure heart so that the unicorn would not be scared.

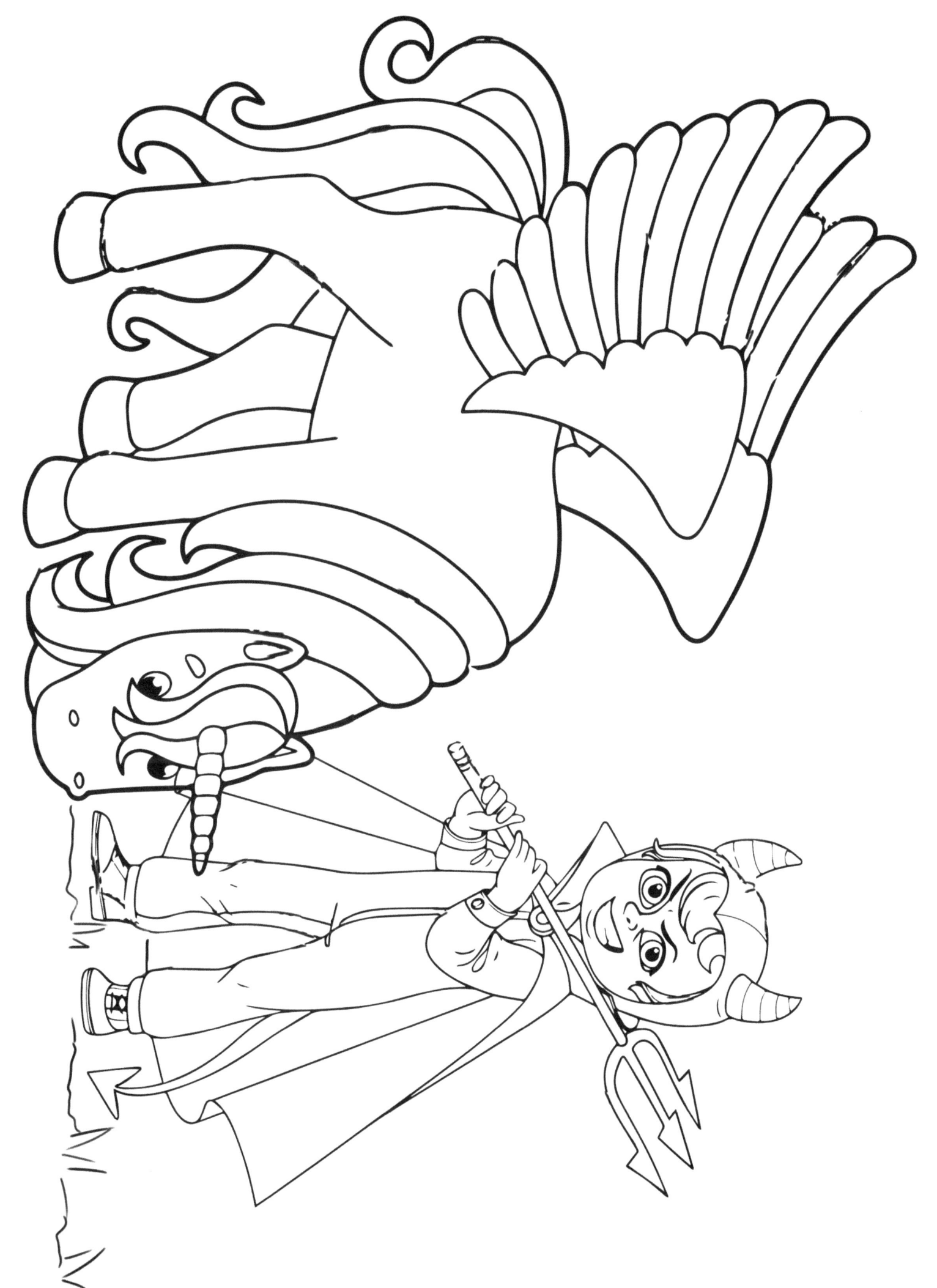

Halloween Fact #6

Illinois grows more than 5 times more pumpkins than any other US state, amounting to more than 500 million pounds of pumpkins per year!

Fun Unicorn Fact #6

Unicorns do not have wings and should not be confused with a Pegasus which is a horse with flying wings.

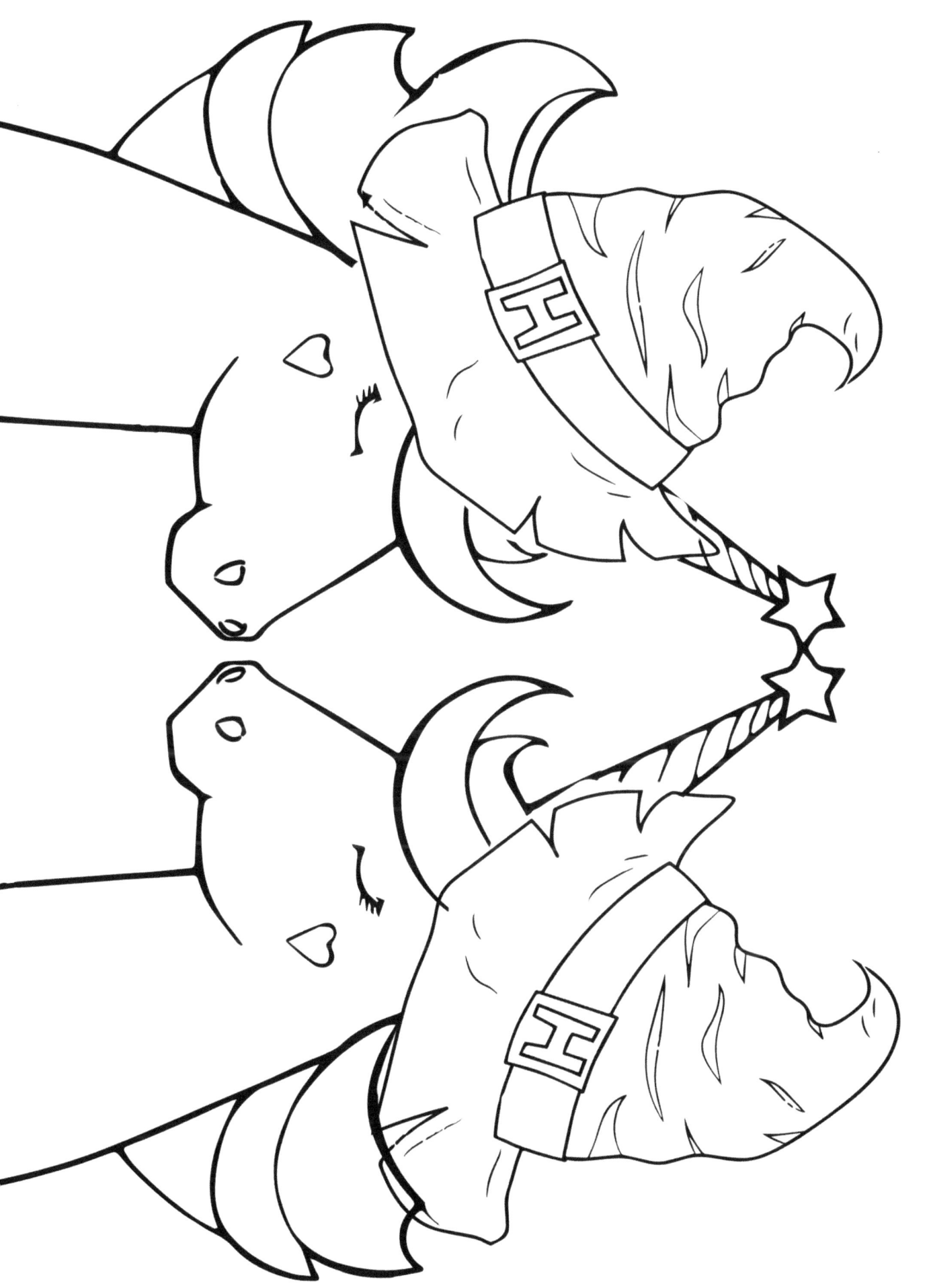

Fun Unicorn Fact #7

Unicorns can eat grass and hay if they choose but it is not necessary since they can absorb energy from the sun.

Fun Unicorn Fact #8

The unicorn is Scotland's national animal.

Congratulations on colouring all the pages!

As a thank you for purchasing this book, enjoy these bonus coloring pages from one of our other unicorn books!

A Message From the Publisher

Hello! My name is Harper and I am the owner of Happy Harper Publishing, the publishing house that brought you this title.

My hope is that your little one loved this book and enjoyed each and every page. If they did, please think about leaving a review for us on Amazon or wherever you purchased this book. It may only take a moment, but it really does mean the world for small businesses like mine.

The mission of Happy Harper is to create premium content for children that will help them learn new things, grow their imaginations, improve their motor skills, and have lots of fun doing it. Without you, however, this would not be possible, so we sincerely thank you for your purchase and for supporting our company mission.

~ Harper

Check out our other books!

For more, visit our Amazon store at:
amazon.com/author/happyharper

www.ingramcontent.com/pod-product-compliance
Ingram Content Group UK Ltd.
Pitfield, Milton Keynes, MK11 3LW, UK
UKHW050416240426
12048UKWH00021B/1548